READY, AIM, INSPIRE!

Ready, Aim, Inspire!

101 Quotes on Leadership & Teamwork

Jim Walker

Writers Club Press
San Jose New York Lincoln Shanghai

Ready, Aim, Inspire!
101 Quotes on Leadership & Teamwork

Writers Club Press
an imprint of iUniverse, Inc.

For information address:
iUniverse, Inc.
5220 S. 16th St., Suite 200
Lincoln, NE 68512
www.iuniverse.com

ISBN: 0-595-24884-5

Printed in the United States of America

Dedicated to

The extraordinary everyday leaders
who lost their lives on 9/11/01,
and to those who now carry on
the enduring fight for freedom

&

My brother Rick,
who leads in his own quiet way

Preface

The events of 9-11 brought into sharp focus the timeless relationship between leadership and service. In just a few shattering hours we were reminded that leadership is not about having the biggest house, the latest technology, the most friends, or the most power—leadership is about serving people in whatever situation life may thrust upon us.

In researching the quotes for this book, I've probably read more about leadership than is healthy—and one thing I can definitely report is that simply reading about leadership will NOT make you a leader. However, that being said, I do believe that these quotes can act as a guide and inspiration for embracing the mantle of leadership.

The criteria for selecting them was a combination of: who said it, what did they say, and how eloquently did they say it? The final selection criteria was my own personal sense of how much did they "ring true"? I hope that you find the results to be worthwhile and inspiring!

Also, if you have a chance, please also visit our website **www.Ready AimInspire.com** where you will find additional resources and quotes. I would also love to hear your own quotes, comments and feedback: **jim.walker@mindpalace.com**

Sincerely,

Jim Walker

He who is greatest among you
shall be your servant;
whoever exalts himself will be humbled,
and whoever humbles himself will be exalted.

—Jesus
as recorded in Matthew 23:11-12

Without training, they lacked knowledge.
Without knowledge, they lacked confidence.
Without confidence, they lacked victory.

—Julius Caesar

You might as well expect the rivers to run backward
as that any man who is born a free man
should be contented
when penned up
and denied liberty
to go where he pleases.

We only ask an even chance
to live as other men live.
We ask to be recognized as men.
Let me be a free man...
free to travel...free to stop...free to work...
free to choose my own teachers...
free to follow the religion of my Fathers...
free to think and talk and act for myself.

—Chief Joseph

I am going to find 36 men
who have the pride
to make any sacrifice to win.
There are such men.
If they're not here, I'll get them.
If you are not one,
if you don't want to play,
you might as well leave right now.

—Vince Lombardi
First day as head coach
of the 1-10-1 Green Bay Packers
July 23rd, 1959

Standing in the middle of the road
is very dangerous;
you get knocked down by the traffic
from both sides.

—Margaret Thatcher

Getting good players is easy.
Getting them to play together
is the hard part.

—Casey Stengel

Strategy without tactics
is the slowest route to victory.
Tactics without strategy
is the noise before defeat.

—Sun Tzu

We will either find a way,
or make one.

—Hannibal

Freedom
is actually a bigger game than power.
Power
is about what you can control.
Freedom
is about what you can unleash.

—Harriet Rubin

Man doesn't know
what he is capable of
until he is asked.

—Kofi Annan

I rode
when no one else would ride,
sometimes not even my teammates.

—Lance Armstrong

You give me the right people,
and I don't much care
what organization you give me.
Good things will happen.

Give the wrong people,
and it doesn't matter
what you do with the organization.
Bad things will happen.

—Colin Powell

You've got me!
…but who's got you?

—Lois Lane to Superman

What you are
shouts so loudly in my ears,
I can't hear what you say.

—Ralph Waldo Emerson

We must indeed all
hang together,
or, most assuredly,
we shall all
hang separately.

—Benjamin Franklin

Despise no man
and consider nothing impossible,
for there is no man who does not have his hour
and there is no thing that does not have its place.

—The Talmud

Children have never been very good
at listening to their elders,
but they have never failed to imitate them.

—James Baldwin

Too often we underestimate the power
of a touch, a smile, a kind word,
a listening ear, an honest compliment,
or the smallest act of caring,
all of which have the potential
to turn a life around.

It's overwhelming to consider
the continuous opportunities
there are to make our love felt.

—Leo Buscaglia

Leadership and learning
are indispensable to each other.

—John F. Kennedy

I am a leader by default,
only because nature
does not allow a vacuum.

—Bishop Desmond Tutu

Leadership is the art
of getting someone else
to do something you want done
because he wants to do it.

—Dwight D. Eisenhower

Michael,
if you can't pass,
you can't play.

—Coach Dean Smith
to Michael Jordan in his freshman year at UNC.

Take a chance!
All life is a chance.
The man who goes furthest
is generally the one
who is willing to do and dare.
The sure thing boat never gets far from shore.

—Dale Carnegie

Example is not the main thing
in influencing others.
It's the only thing.

—Dr. Albert Schweitzer

The final test of a leader
is that they leave behind them
in other people
the conviction and the will
to carry on.

—Walter Lippmann

Leadership consists not in degrees of technique
but in traits of character;
it requires moral
rather than athletic or intellectual effort,
and it imposes on both leader and follower alike
the burdens of self-restraint.

—Lewis H. Lapham

Leaders who win the respect of others
are the ones who
deliver more than they promise,
not the ones who
promise more than they can deliver.

—Mark A. Clement

He who has great power
should use it lightly.

—Seneca

Exceptional leaders cultivate the Merlin-like habit
of acting in the present moment
as ambassadors of a radically different future,
in order to imbue their organizations
with a breakthrough vision
of what it is possible to achieve.

—Charles E. Smith

You have brains in your head.
You have feet in your shoes.
You can steer yourself
any direction you choose.

—Dr. Seuss

A boat doesn't go forward
if each one is rowing their own way.

—Swahili proverb

When you feel grateful,
you become great,
and eventually attract great things.

—Plato

The individual activity
of one man with backbone
will do more than a thousand men
with a mere wishbone.

—William J.H. Boetcker

I not only use all the brains I have,
but all that I can borrow.

—Woodrow Wilson

It is the nature of man
to rise to greatness
if greatness is expected of him.

—John Steinbeck

The scientific management (stomach) paradigm
says, "Pay me well."
The human relations (heart) paradigm
says, "Treat me well."
The human resource (mind) paradigm
suggests, "Use me well."

The principle-centered leadership (whole person)
paradigm says:
"Let's talk about vision and mission, roles, and goals.
I want to make a meaningful contribution."

—Stephen Covey
Principle Centered Leadership

The function of leadership
is to produce more leaders,
not more followers.

—Ralph Nader

A good leader
is not the person who does things right,
but the person who finds
the right things to do.

—Anthony S. Dadovano

Leader—
a dealer in hope.

—Napoleon

The best way to get people to think out of the box
is not to create the box
in the first place.

—Martin Cooper
Inventor of the cel-phone

To lead the people,
walk behind them.

—Lao Tzu

When the correct direction is hard to discern,
action is better than hesitation.
That doesn't mean heedlessly making
sweeping changes.
But rather than freezing
in the headlights of oncoming change,
you can at least
explore, experiment, and perhaps learn
what's coming down the pike.

—Rosabeth Moss Kanter

When old words die out on the tongue,
new melodies break forth from the heart;
and where the old tracks are lost,
new country is revealed with its wonders.

—Rabindranath Tagore

If I were to wish for anything,
I should not wish for wealth and power,
but for the passionate sense of potential,
for the eye, which, ever young and ardent,
sees the possible.
What wine is so sparkling,
so fragrant,
so intoxicating,
as possibility!

—Søren Kierkegaard

The greatest oak
was once a little nut
who held its ground.

—anon

Everyone thinks of changing the world,
but no one thinks of changing themselves.

—Leo Tolstoy

Blessed are the people whose leaders
can look destiny in the eye
without flinching,
but also without attempting to play God.

—Henry Kissinger

Spread love everywhere you go:
first of all in your own house.
Give love to your children, to your wife or husband,
to a next door neighbor…
Let no one ever come to you
without leaving better and happier.
Be the living expression of God's kindness;
kindness in your face,
kindness in your eyes,
kindness in your smile,
kindness in your warm greeting.

—Mother Theresa

We must adjust to changing times
and still hold to unchanging principles.

—Jimmy Carter

Outstanding leaders go out of their way
to boost the self-esteem of their personnel.
If people believe in themselves,
it's amazing what they can accomplish.

—Sam Walton

The great leaders are like the best conductors—
they reach beyond the notes
to reach the magic in the players.

—Blaine Lee

An army of a thousand is easy to find,
but, ah, how difficult
to find a general.

—Chinese proverb

A frightened captain
makes a frightened crew.

—Lister Sinclair

It is much safer
to obey
than to rule.

—Thomas a Kempis

To obtain measurably superior results in the workplace,
managers must understand
why people behave as they do with the same depth
that rocket scientists understand gravity.

—Aubrey C. Daniels
Bringing Out the Best In People

And when we think we lead,
we are most led.

—Lord Byron

A true leader
always keeps an element of surprise
up his sleeve,
which others cannot grasp
but which keeps his public
excited and breathless.

—Charles de Gaulle

The right person
appears
at the right time.

—Italian proverb

If you think you can do a thing
or that you cannot do a thing,
in either case you are right.

—Henry Ford

Be willing to make decisions.
That's the most important quality
in a good leader.
Don't fall victim to what I call
the ready aim-aim-aim-aim syndrome.

—T. Boone Pickens

Alone we can do so little;
together we can do so much.

—Helen Keller

When building a team,
I always search first
for people who love to win.
If I can't find any of those,
I look for people who hate to lose.

—H. Ross Perot

Find something you love to do
and you'll never have to work
a day in your life.

—Harvey Mackay

Alone, all alone.
Nobody, but nobody
Can make it out here alone.

—Maya Angelou

Much can be done
by taking friends out for rides.

—Carl Benz
Founder, Mercedes-Benz

When leadership is not the province
of a few hundred noblemen,
or a few thousand big landholders and shareholders,
but is shared among an aristocracy of achievement
numbering in the millions,
decision making is not done by a club
but by a crowd.
So the core issue of executive leadership
is a paradox of participation:
How do you get everybody in on the act
and still get things done?

—Harlan Cleveland

When nothing seems to help,
I go and look at a stonecutter
hammering away at his rock
perhaps a hundred times
without as much as a crack showing in it.
Yet at the hundred and first blow it will split in two,
and I know it was not that blow that did it—
but all that had gone before.

—Jacob Riis

I must study politics and war
that my sons may have liberty
to study mathematics and philosophy.

—John Adams

The hope of a secure and livable world
lies with disciplined nonconformists
who are dedicated to
justice, peace and brotherhood.

—Martin Luther King, Jr.

The path to greatness
is along with others.

—Baltasar Gracion

A group becomes a team
when each member is sure enough of himself
and his contribution
to praise the skills of the others.

—Norman Shilde

Hell, there are no rules here—
we're trying to accomplish something.

—Thomas Edison

It is not the critic who counts,
not the man who points out how the strong man stumbled, or where
the doer of deeds could have done better.

The credit belongs to the man
who is actually in the arena;
whose face is marred by the dust and sweat and blood;
who strives valiantly;
who errs and comes short again and again;
who knows the great enthusiasms, the great devotions
and spends himself in a worthy course; who at the best,
knows in the end the triumph of high achievement,
and who, at worst, if he fails,
at least fails while daring greatly;
so that his place shall never be
with those cold and timid souls
who know neither victory or defeat.

—Theodore Roosevelt

Leaders are visionaries
with a poorly developed sense of fear
and no concept of the odds against them.

—Robert Jarvik

Do not follow where the path may lead.
Go instead where there is no path
and leave a trail.

—Ralph Waldo Emerson

Praise does wonders
for our sense of hearing.

—Arnold H. Glasgow

When I see people pulling back from taking risks,
risks that perhaps they know they should be taking—
my experience is that it's rarely
because they're afraid of failing.
Most of the time it's because
they're afraid of succeeding.

What I mean is—when we become good risk-takers,
we often find ourselves
in positions of increasing responsibility.

—John Graham
President, Giraffe Project

A team is a team is a team.
Shakespeare said that many times.

—Dan Devine

A nation will find it very hard
to look up
to the leaders
who are keeping their ears
to the ground.

—Winston Churchill

Leadership is about solving problems.
The day soldiers stop bringing you their problems
is the day you have stopped leading them.
They have either lost confidence that you can help
or concluded you do not care.
Either case is a failure of leadership.

—Colin Powell

Though God hath raised me high,
yet this I count the glory of my crown:
that I have reigned with your loves.
And though you have had, and may have,
many mightier and wiser princes sitting in this seat;
yet you never had, nor shall have any
that will love you better.

—Queen Elizabeth I

As long as you keep a person down,
some part of you has to be down there
to hold the person down,
so it means you cannot soar
as you otherwise might.

—Marian Anderson

Once convinced
that a particular course of action
is the correct one,
a leader must be undaunted
when the going gets tough.

—President Ronald Reagan

Instead of nurturing talent,
encouraging people to learn
from mistakes and successes,
organizations all too often
ignore leadership potential,
offer no relevant training or role models,
and punish those who make small errors
while trying to lead.

Individuals, too, get in their own way
by failing to assess
their developmental needs realistically
and to proactively seek means of meeting those needs.

—John Kotter
What Leaders Really Do

There are only five or six big plays
in every game,
and you have to make them to win.
In a time of crisis, it is absolutely imperative.

—Vince Lombardi

Those who dance
are considered insane
by those
who cannot hear the music.

—George Carlin

Never hire or promote in your own image.
It is foolish to replicate your strength
and idiotic to replicate your weakness.
It is essential to employ, trust, and reward
those whose perspective, ability, and judgment
are radically different from yours.
It is also rare,
for it requires uncommon
humility, tolerance, and wisdom.

—Dee W. Hock
Founder of Visa

If you tell people where to go,
but not how to get there,
you'll be amazed at the results.

—Gen. George S. Patton

The harder the conflict,
the more glorious the triumph.
What we obtain too cheap,
we esteem too lightly;
it is dearness only that gives everything its value.
I love the man that can smile in trouble,
that can gather strength from distress
and grow brave.

—Thomas Paine

I desire to so conduct the affairs
of this administration that if at the end,
when I come to lay down the reins of power,
I have lost every other friend on earth,
I shall at least have one friend left,
and that friend shall be down inside of me.

—Abraham Lincoln

Good leaders make people feel
that they're at the very heart of things,
not at the periphery.
Everyone feels that he or she makes a difference
to the success of the organization.
When that happens people feel centered
and that gives their work meaning.

—Warren Bennis

The majority of men meet with failure
because of their lack of persistence
in creating new plans
to take the place
of those which fail.

—Napoleon Hill

The flames kindled on the Fourth of July, 1776,
have spread over too much of the globe
to be extinguished
by the feeble engines of despotism;
on the contrary,
they will consume these engines
and all who work them.

—Thomas Jefferson to John Adams, 1821

Action springs not from thought,
but from a readiness for responsibility.

—Dietrich Bonhoeffer

"We saw no sign of fear in him.
Watching him made men of us.
Marching or fighting, he was leading.
We followed him
because there was nothing else to do".

Thousands of Americans
were spilled onto Omaha Beach.
The high ground was won
by a handful of men like Taylor
who on that day burned with a flame
bright beyond common understanding.

Description of Lieutenant Walter Taylor by
Staff Sergeant Frank Price

Recorded by combat historian S.L.A. Marshall
The Atlantic Monthly; November 1960
First Wave at Omaha Beach

Are you guys ready?
Let's roll!

—Todd Beamer
Flight 93
9.11.01

I don't know what your destiny will be,
but one thing I know;
the only ones among you
who will be really happy
are those who will have
sought and found
how to serve.

—Dr. Albert Schweitzer

Civil disobedience
becomes a sacred duty
when the State becomes
lawless and corrupt.

—Mahatma Gandhi

Never give in—
never, never, never, never,
in nothing great or small,
large or petty,
never give in
except to convictions of honour and good sense.
Never yield to force;
never yield
to the apparently overwhelming might of the enemy.

—Winston Churchill
speaking at Harrow School,
October 29th, 1941

Some men give up their designs
when they have almost reached the goal;
while others, on the contrary,
obtain a victory by exerting,
at the last moment,
more vigorous efforts than ever before.

—Herodotus

Where there is no vision,
the people perish.

Proverbs 29:18

About the Author

Jim Walker is a writer, teacher, and web consultant living in Philadelphia, Pennsylvania with his wife and children. If you have comments about this book, or have quotes to share,
please e-Mail him at:
jim.walker@MindPalace.com

Additional leadership resources can be found at:
www.readyaiminspire.com

0-595-24884-5

Printed in the United States
105160LV00005B/220/A

9 780595 248841